evolution

elizabeth eyre

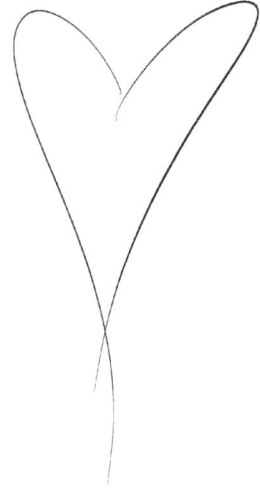

Content Warning

This collection covers themes of violence, abuse, self-harm & generational trauma.

If you or somebody you know have experienced any of the above, please seek specialist support.

evolution

/ˌiːvəˈluːʃ(ə)n, ˈɛvəluːʃ(ə)n/

noun

the gradual development of something

transmute

your embrace

        something akin to valium

        firm

            calming

                addictive

your anger

        makes something near my heart

            quaver with fear

        makes my heart ...

                ache

until the valium

            returns

you taught me how to love myself

      : false prophecy :

words designed

to attach

entwine

secure

thereupon when your truth emerges

i am blinded by your voice

and i only doubt myself

Elizabeth Eyre

your eyes

always tell me

the truth

you hate me for it

your words

betrayed by your actions

frame your hypocrite

i know him well

i have been tiptoeing through your tulips for days

Elizabeth Eyre

i cannot take it any longer

i don't deserve this! - HEAR ME

the pot of coffee

smashes against the wall

we scream

we rage

we tire

we talk

within a day you've forgotten what we said

you forget your apology

you forget your promises

you only remember my anger

cold indifference

rage

(nothing in-between)

sanctimonious judgement

how long since you smiled last

did i ever make you happy?

does ***anything*** make you happy?

Elizabeth Eyre

i tripped

why didn't you put your hands out?

i don't know

she raises her eyebrow

purses her lips

but continues with her examination

it's only a mild concussion, but we need to send you home with somebody who will watch you for the next few days

you take me home

you apologise

the next two days you are

so kind

so loving

so contrite

i believe you

turn the heat high

until a hell torrent

rains down

combining with

acrid tears on her cheeks

                                                burn away the shame

Elizabeth Eyre

i, the first chair

in the orchestra

of your pain

you conduct me through

your every thought

reliving your past

every

single

day

her smile was systematic

perfectly constructed to portray happiness

nobody saw the terror in her chin

she had the nose of a champion boxer

self-straightened too many times

nobody noticed

the knives had all been hidden

Elizabeth Eyre

my song comes on

you laugh

i press skip

hiding another piece

of me

your head

crying in my lap

droplets of blood

from my freshly broken nose

force their way

through the towel, into your hair

"it's okay… i know you didn't mean it"

i stroke your head the way you like

your breathing slows

my silent tears increase

i rearrange my screaming body

and reach for a fresh towel

my brain numb to all feeling

am i concussed again?

or just too tired to feel

Elizabeth Eyre

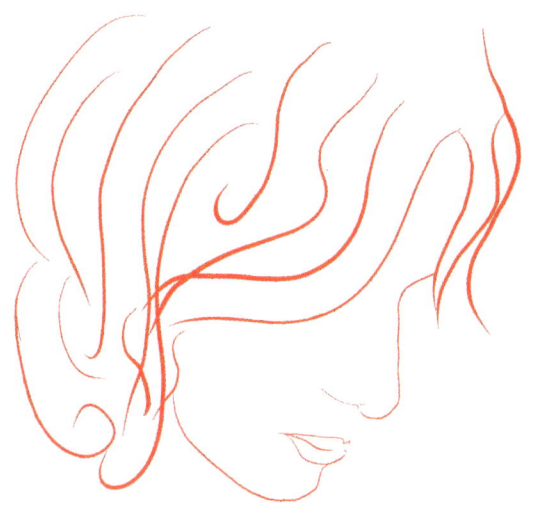

fuck you

Elizabeth Eyre

anger

and cruel words

on the days you are too sick to get out of bed

it's not your fault

you don't mean what you say

it's not your fault

you are in pain

it's not your fault

you are hurting

it's not your fault

you will forget what you said by tomorrow

it's not your fault

it is my fault

i don't know how

to make you happy

Elizabeth Eyre

i'm sorry

saya minta maaf

je suis désolé

es tut mir leid

lo siento

tha mi duilich

ごめんなさい

doleo

e kala mai ia'u

mae'n ddrwg gennyf

Λυπάμαι

אני מצטער

对不起

žao mi je

to mi je líto

i am sorry

i apologise

it never matters how i say it

i wait for water fountain wishes

i wait for the falling stars

i wait for the if onlys

i wait for the next broken promise

if you can't love me at my worst

you don't deserve me at my best

~ i believed you ~

startle

fly

freeze

fight

fly

cry

breathe

rinse and repeat as required

Elizabeth Eyre

you studied my cracks and sharp edges

you poured the gold

between my pieces

you informed me i was this new shape

a more beautiful version of myself

you told me it celebrated my flaws

as the gold tarnished

your smile faded

new cracks formed

some from life

some from you

some self-inflicted

you hate me for them

you blame them on the old cracks

i'm sorry

i used to tell the story of soulmates:

beings torn apart by the gods

i told people it was our story

i thought it was our story

now i see

our story was more...

                      shakespearean

more akin

    to kate

        & petruchio

grateful

    it was not

        romeo

            & juliet

Elizabeth Eyre

even your compliments have thorns

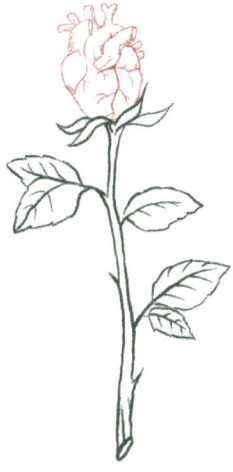

he pushes things back inside my arm

and starts to sew

he does not care

not for my stuttering excuses

not for my tears

he does not hear my silent screams

ADMIT ME

he has seen much worse tonight

he turns to you

can you take care of her at home?

you nod and say something he approves of

i can't hear you

why can he hear you?

but he cannot hear me screaming

                  SAVE ME

Elizabeth Eyre

your
sanctimonious
judgment
is
never
satiated

when the bruises fade

    but

        the

            tears

                remain

how long till we

    forget again

Elizabeth Eyre

Elizabeth Eyre

emergence

Elizabeth Eyre

i stare through the glass

the world keeps passing by

i am no more significant to them

than the birds on the wires

so i sit

and watch

and wait

i wait

to hear you

to feel you

to know you...

          again

your words still tumble through my mind

the urge to defend myself rises in my chest

the lack of justice

overwhelms my sensibilities

anger eludes me

i ran out of tears many moons ago

you have left me with nothing

a shell of myself

desperately trying to find myself

in shallow chores

and unwritten words

which clatter around my hollow chest

Elizabeth Eyre

how

do you still control

my thoughts

my actions

my beliefs

how

do you still control

me

i would sell my soul

to no longer dream of you

to forget you

to lose you

to love you no longer

Elizabeth Eyre

sometimes

as i lie here

i feel your arms

around me once more

i feel your breath

where my neck meets my collar bone

i hear your words whispering in my ear

you're a beautiful woman

i love you

LIAR

we have been gone

for so long

my nerves don't believe me yet

i feel like i am cheating on you

when i went on a date

i feel shame when i sing

i have to double check you are not here

i feel guilt when i think of you alone

it feels better than fear

Elizabeth Eyre

the voice in my head

is yours

it has the judgement

of fire

and brimstone

trash begins to resemble treasure

i don't want them

i had only ever wanted us

i ramble

i rant

i devour

empty calories

whilst pinching my fat

i do not need you to torture me

i have had decades to perfect that job myself

the dysfunctionality

we are all frauds and masochists

never good enough for ourselves

Elizabeth Eyre

hunting and gathering dopamine

the only ways we can

liars

      ...every one of us

every little deceit eating at our psyches

the most destructive of all...

            'i am well, thank you!'"

they all have the same red flags

that they see in me

Elizabeth Eyre

i already escaped my hell

i will not accept delivery of yours

Elizabeth Eyre

everybody i meet

seems as broken as me

we are all

too old

too tired

too broken

i retire before anything begins

do thoughts of me

flicker across your mind?

or do they burn through your synapses?

Elizabeth Eyre

when she dies

blackness envelops my mind,

thoughts float on the horizon

i grasp for them

desperately

i need a thought

a single word even

without words i no longer feel me

inside this body i call mine

suddenly

every muscle in my body

awakens in unison

HIM

i want him

i want

his arms enveloping me

his scent

his words

whispering from his lips

convincing me

it will be okay

i cannot

that part of you exists momentarily

and i no longer have the capacity

to justify the rest of you

alone in my grief

i surrender

to the aches

the clouds

the embodiment of surrealism

Elizabeth Eyre

i pine

my grief for their deaths

allows me to grieve the loss of us

finally

the sigh escapes my chest

it does not ask permission

tears fall unnoticed till their salt reaches my sigh

isolation encompasses my entire being

the nights grow colder without you

i see the frost grow thicker

the mist hangs lower, and longer

it's the kind of cold that burns your bones

i have grown colder without you

but i am happy

Elizabeth Eyre

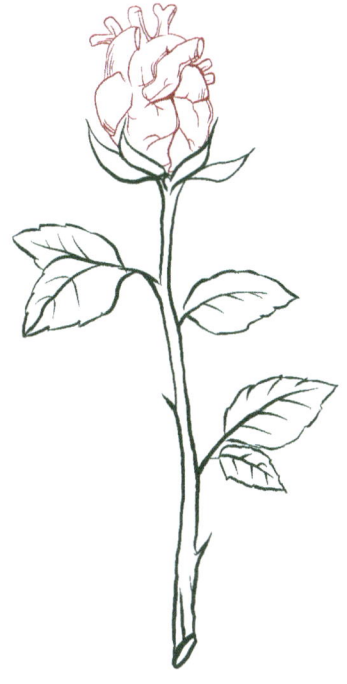

About the Author

Elizabeth is a proud woolwonga woman, who spent her childhood in South East Queensland hiding in the frangipani to read Harry Potter and write love poems.

Elizabeth now lives in lutruwita and feels the ice, and wind running through her veins, embracing her heart. Her soul has found its home amongst the she-oak and wattles.

Copyright © 2022 by Elizabeth Eyre

All rights reserved. No part of this book may be used or reproduced in any form whatsoever without written permission except in the case of brief quotations in critical articles or reviews.

http://www.elizabetheyre.com

ELIZABETH_EYRE_

ISBN - Paperback: 978-0-6455576-0-2
ISBN - EPUBk : 978-0-6455576-1-9
First Edition: 2022

www.ingramcontent.com/pod-product-compliance
Lightning Source LLC
Chambersburg PA
CBHW040244010526
44107CB00065B/2865